Key Stage 2

Grammar

R P & HOME LEARNING

NAPE — National Association for Primary Education

Contents

AUTHOR: Camilla de la Bédoyère
EDITORIAL: John Cattermole, Vicky Garrard, Julia Rolf
DESIGN: Jen Bishop, Dave Jones
ILLUSTRATORS: Bridget Dowty, Sarah Wimperis
PRODUCTION: Chris Herbert, Claire Walker

COMMISSIONING EDITOR: Polly Willis
PUBLISHER AND CREATIVE DIRECTOR: Nick Wells

3 Book Pack ISBN 1-84451-087-5   Book ISBN 1-84451-044-1
6 Book Pack ISBN 1-84451-090-5   Book ISBN 1-04451-099-9

First published in 2004

A copy of the CIP data for this book is available from the British Library upon request.

Created and produced by
FLAME TREE PUBLISHING
Crabtree Hall,
Crabtree Lane,
Fulham, London SW6 6TY
United Kingdom
www.flametreepublishing.com

Flame Tree Publishing is part of The Foundry Creative Media Co. Ltd.

© The Foundry Creative Media Co. Ltd, 2004

Printed in Croatia

Foreword

Sometimes when I am crossing the playground on my way to visit a primary school I pass young children playing at schools. There is always a stern authoritarian little teacher at the front laying down the law to the unruly group of children in the pretend class. This puzzles me a little because the school I am visiting is very far from being like the children's play. Where do they get this Victorian view of what school is like? Perhaps it's handed down from generation to generation through the genes. Certainly they don't get it from their primary school. Teachers today are more often found alongside their pupils, who are learning by actually doing things for themselves, rather than merely listening and obeying instructions.

Busy children, interested and involved in their classroom reflect what we know about how they learn. Of course they learn from teachers but most of all they learn from their experience of life and their life is spent both in and out of school. Indeed, if we compare the impact upon children of even the finest schools and teachers, we find that three or four times as great an impact is made by the reality of children's lives outside the school. That reality has the parent at the all important centre. No adult can have so much impact, for good or ill, as the young child's mother or father.

This book, and others in the series, are founded on the sure belief that the great majority of parents want to help their children grow and learn and that teachers are keen to support them. The days when parents were kept at arm's length from schools are long gone and over the years we have moved well beyond the white line painted on the playground across which no parent must pass without an appointment. Now parents move freely in and out of schools and very often are found in the classrooms backing up the teachers. Both sides of the partnership know how important it is that children should be challenged and stimulated both in and out of school.

Perhaps the most vital part of this book is where parents and children are encouraged to develop activities beyond those offered on the page. The more the children explore and use the ideas and techniques we want them to learn, the more they will make new knowledge of their very own. It's not just getting the right answer, it's growing as a person through gaining skill in action and not only in books. The best way to learn is to live.

I remember reading a story to a group of nine year old boys. The story was about soldiers and of course the boys, bloodthirsty as ever, were hanging on my every word. I came to the word khaki and I asked the group "What colour is khaki?" One boy was quick to answer. "Silver" he said, "It's silver." "Silver? I queried. "Yes," he said with absolute confidence, "silver, my Dad's car key is silver." Now I reckon I'm a pretty good teller of stories to children but when it came down to it, all my dramatic reading of a gripping story gave way immediately to the power of the boy's experience of life. That meant so much more to him, as it does to all children.

JOHN COE
General Secretary, National Association for Primary Education (NAPE).

Parents and teachers work together in NAPE to improve the quality of learning and teaching in primary schools. We campaign hard for a better deal for children at the vital early stage of their education upon which later success depends. We are always pleased to hear from parents.

NAPE, Moulton College, Moulton, Northampton, NN3 7RR,
Telephone: 01604 647 646 Web: www.nape.org.uk

Grammar is one of six books in the **Revision, Practice & Home Learning** series, which has been devised to help you support your child as they prepare for their SATs at the end of Year Six.

The book contains revision notes to remind your child of the essential elements of good grammar and it can guide you, the parent, through part of the National Literacy Framework. This Framework identifies the need for children to learn reading and writing skills at three different levels; word, sentence and text. The balance between these levels is important; the **Spelling** book in the series should be studied in conjunction with **Grammar**.

Each page contains revision notes, exercises for your child to complete and practical pointers to give you extra information and guidance (**Parents Start Here**). There is also an **Activity** box with each topic which will offer your child activities to carry out once the book has been put away. Many of these focus on the third part of the Literacy Strategy; Speaking and Listening. At the end of the book you will find a checklist of topics – you can use this to mark off each topic as it is mastered.

This book has been designed for children to work through alone; but it is recommended that you read the book first to acquaint yourself with the material it contains. Try to be at hand when your child is working with the book; your input is valuable.

Encourage good study habits in your child:

- Try to set aside a short time every day for studying. Ten to 20 minutes a day is plenty.

- Give your child access to drinking water whenever they work; research suggests this helps them perform better.

- Reward your child; plenty of praise for good work motivates children to succeed.

- Revisit topics regularly to help reinforce long term memory patterns.

This book is intended to support your child in their school work. Sometimes children find particular topics hard to understand; discuss this with their teacher, who may be able to suggest alternative ways to help your child.

Parents Start Here...

Your child was first taught about the grammatical functions of words, such as nouns, in Key Stage One. By this stage children should have a very firm concept of what a noun is and be able to recognise them.

Nouns

Remember!

- Nouns are naming words.
- Common nouns name things, e.g. books, pigs, pins.
- Common nouns also name abstract things, e.g. beauty, thought, faith.
- Proper nouns name people or places, e.g. Santa Claus, Lapland, Peter, Megan.
- Proper nouns must always start with a capital letter.

1. Underline all the common nouns and circle all of the proper nouns:

I do not understand why my daughter, Maggie, cannot put her dirty laundry into the basket. Every day I go into her bedroom and I never know what I will find. On Tuesday Maggie had left a wet towel on the carpet, which was soggy and smelly by Wednesday. On Thursday I found an old mug under Maggie's bed. It was harbouring some fungus, I think. I've had a good idea, though. I am sending Maggie to work for Joyce, a friend of mine who runs a cleaning company. Hopefully she will get the hint.

2. Write the name of the country that goes with each word, e.g. French = France:

a) Danish _____

b) Swedish _____

c) Russian _____

d) Welsh _____

e) Irish _____

f) Italian _____

g) Chinese _____

h) South African _____

i) Austrian _____

j) Spanish _____

3. Write a sentence which contains at least one proper noun:

_____

_____

4. Write the names of 5 nouns; they could be things you can see around you now:

1. _____

2. _____

3. _____

4. _____

5. _____

TRY THIS

Activity

Listen to a radio play (try Radio Four). Listen carefully to how the actors help create an atmosphere just using their voices and your imagination.

Check Your Progress!

Nouns ☐

Turn to page 48 and put a tick next to what you have just learned.

Top Tip!
Remember to give your child lots of praise – they will work so much better.

Parents Start Here...

Encourage your child to draw up a list of good adjectives as they come across them. Creating and using a word bank like this will help your child's creative writing enormously.

Adjectives

Remember!

- Adjectives are describing words.
- Adjectives tell us more about the nouns in a sentence.
- Numbers can be adjectives.
- Adjectives help to create a picture and spice up writing.

1. Circle the adjectives:

a) The cranky old woman shook her knobbly stick at me.

b) When the wooden desk collapsed my porcelain mug smashed.

c) Tom is lazy but his sister is messy.

d) Pink cars, pink hats, pink slippers; you name it my sister has it, just as long as it is pink.

2. Add some adjectives to make these sentences more interesting:

a) The strawberries were tasty.

_____

b) The Moon looks big.

_____

c) Dragons have long tails.

_____

d) The bucket leaks.

_____

3. Change the adjective 'nice' for a better one:

a) My Granny's dog is nice.

_____

b) My new teacher is nice.

_____

c) The view from the cliff was nice.

_____

4. Look in a dictionary to discover the meaning of the adjective 'narcissistic'. Write the meaning here:

_____

_____

_____

 Activity

Discover the story of Narcissus. You will find it on the Internet or in the library. Look under 'Greek Mythology'.

Check Your Progress!
Adjectives
Turn to page 48 and put a tick next to what you have just learned.

Parents Start Here...

Listen to your child read aloud. At this age children usually read alone, but it is important that children can read aloud in an entertaining manner.

Verbs

Remember!

- Verbs are doing, or being words.
- Every sentence has a verb.
- Verbs can tell you when something happened; they may describe an action in the past, present or future. This is the verb's tense.

1. Read each sentence and underline the verbs:

a) Sebastian blew hard into his trumpet, making a loud but tuneful noise.

b) As the periscope was raised the captain slipped his glasses on to his nose.

c) She plucked the rose deftly from the stem, tearing her skin on a prickly thorn.

d) The hunter peered through the trees and spotted the cheetah lying beneath a low branch.

2. Use these being verbs in sentences of your own:

a) love

_____

b) loathe

3. Find the verb in each sentence and decide whether it is describing an action in the past, present or future. Circle the correct answer:

a) The flame flickered in the breeze.   past   present   future

b) I will go to the shop tomorrow, not today.   past   present   future

c) Dad had his lunch in the pub.   past   present   future

d) Mike plays golf every Sunday.   past   present   future

e) The shoots will appear in May or June.   past   present   future

4. Complete the sentences using the correct being verb:

is   were   was   will be

a) The Romans _____ good at inventing things.

b) Elizabeth I _____ a proud and successful queen.

c) On my next birthday I _____ 11.

d) My boyfriend's name _____ Malcolm.

 Activity

Find some new ways to say 'said' in your stories, e.g. uttered, declared, shouted, whispered. Keep a record of the best ones and you can build a word-bank which you can use when you are writing.

Check Your Progress!

Verbs ☐

Turn to page 48 and put a tick next to what you have just learned.

9

Parents Start Here...

Your child may encounter new words in this book. Help them find the definitions in the dictionary and write them into their word bank.

Adverbs

Remember!

- Adverbs tell us about verbs and how something is done.
- Many adverbs end in –ly, e.g. quickly.
- Fast and well are two common adverbs that do not end in –ly.

1. Circle the adverbs:

a) The naughty boys ran quickly down the lane.

b) Stars shine brightly in the night sky.

c) He kissed her tenderly.

d) Tom kicked the door angrily.

e) I rode my bike well.

2. Write a sentence using the adverb 'modestly':

_____

3. Use this chart to turn the adjectives below into adverbs:

Words	What to add	Example
Adjectives (most)	ly	deeply
Words ending in l	ly	beautifully
Words ending in le	remove e then add y	singly
Words ending in y	remove y then add ily	readily

a) wonderful _____

b) possible _____

c) original _____

d) wise _____

e) happy _____

f) simple _____

g) nice _____

Activity

'Modest' is an adjective. Find some alternative words you might use for 'modest'. Look in a thesaurus.

Check Your Progress!

Adverbs

Turn to page 48 and put a tick next to what you have just learned.

Parents Start Here...

When revising it is important to re-visit topics already covered. Before moving on to pronouns, check that your child is able to identify verbs, adverbs, nouns, adjectives and prepositions.

Prepositions

Remember!

● Prepositions tell us the position of one thing in relation to another.
● Prepositions can tell us how things are related in position, e.g. above, beside.
● Prepositions can tell us how things are related in time, e.g. before, during.
● Prepositions can tell us about direction, e.g. towards, into.

1. Underline all the prepositions you can find:

The ancient Indian Snake Charmer sat upon his lavishly embroidered cushion. There were tiny silver bells sewn around the edges of the cushion and they tinkled every time he moved. Before him was a large raffia basket. Inside the basket something moved. The Snake Charmer looked beneath the lid and leapt back in surprise...

2. Identify key parts of each sentence. The first one has been done for you:

a) The man walked towards the hill.

Noun (2): man, hill   Verb: walked   Preposition: towards

b) The young frog leapt over the lily-pad.

Noun (2): _____ _____ Verb: _____

Adjective: _____ Preposition: _____

c) Fluffy was buried next to the new shed.

Proper noun: _____   Noun: _____

Verb: _____   Adjective: _____

Preposition: _____

d) The goblins dug below the mountain.

Noun (2): _____   _____

Verb: _____   Preposition: _____

e) The train came noisily out of the dark, gloomy tunnel.

Noun (2): _____   _____

Verb: _____   Adverb: _____

Adjective (2): _____   _____

Preposition: _____

3. Write a sentence using the preposition during.

_____

_____

_____

TRY THIS

Activity

Write your own news item and present it to your family. You will need to speak clearly and concisely. When journalists tell you about news they have to state the facts; they do not give their opinions. Try to use prepositions of time, e.g. yesterday, before, during, after, etc.

Check Your Progress!

Prepositions ☐

Turn to page 48 and put a tick next to what you have just learned.

Parents Start Here...

Your child may not see the point of being able to identify and name the parts of a sentence. Grammar is now considered an integral part of the curriculum because it enables readers to better understand texts and become good writers themselves.

Pronouns

Remember!

- Pronouns are words we use instead of nouns.
- Pronouns help to keep writing and speech flowing.
- Common pronouns include them, we, it, he, they, I, you, etc.

1. Write out the sentences but replace the nouns, where appropriate, with pronouns.

a) My name is John and John am 10 years old.

_____

b) I stamped on the dolly so hard the dolly broke.

_____

c) Harriet is my sister and Harriet often teases me.

_____

d) The pigeons flew overhead and the pigeons made a terrible noise.

_____

e) The horrid boy chewed his gum then the horrid boy spat his gum on to the road.

_____

2. Write sentences using the following pronouns:

a) him _____

_____

b) us _____

_____

c) me _____

_____

d) he _____

_____

e) you _____

_____

 Activity

The next time adults are talking about something you don't really understand, ask them questions politely. You should be able get the information you need to follow what they are saying. You can pretend you are a journalist finding out the facts.

Check Your Progress!

Pronouns ☐

Turn to page 48 and put a tick next to what you have just learned.

Parents Start Here...

Keep a watchful eye on your child's handwriting. They should be joining all of the letters in a word, except capitals. They will gain marks in the SATs for legible, joined-up writing.

Conjunctions And Articles

Remember!

- Conjunctions are words we use to join two parts of a sentence (phrases) together, e.g. because, and, but.
- Conjunctions can also be used to join two sentences together.
- Conjunctions help your writing flow and add meaning.
- There are two types of article; the is a definite article, an, a and some are all indefinite articles.

1. Underline the conjunctions in these sentences:

a) My brother was late because the bus broke down.

b) I took my keys and got into the car.

c) The teacher told the children to be quiet but they carried on talking.

d) I cannot go home until my Mum calls me.

e) The firework will not explode if it gets wet.

2. Change these two sentences into one, using a conjunction:

Betty roasted the lamb. She boiled the potatoes.

3. Circle the correct article:

a) The / A shopping trolley had a broken wheel and toppled over.

b) My sister ate a / an orange.

c) The man wanted to find a / some fossils.

4. Circle all of the articles in this passage:

> As the children emerged through the silvery cloud they saw an amazing sight. Some sparks of light flew around their heads and, as a gentle breeze tickled their faces, a golden face appeared in front of them.

Activity

Use a tape recorder to record your voice when you are telling a story or reading aloud. Does your voice show emotion? Is it interesting to listen to? Would you enjoy listening to yourself?

Check Your Progress!
Conjunctions And Articles
Turn to page 48 and put a tick next to what you have just learned.

Top Tip!
Remember to give your child lots of praise – they will work so much better.

Parents Start Here...

Ask your child to identify different types of sentence in the book they are currently reading.

Statements, Questions And Imperatives

Remember!

- Questions are sentences that require an answer.
- Questions end with a question mark, e.g. Why are you crying?
- Statements are questions that tell you a fact, e.g. you are crying.
- An imperative is a sentence that contains an order or is being expressed with urgency, e.g. You're crying! Stop crying now!

1. Mark each sentence as:
   a question (Q)
   an imperative (I)
   or a statement (S)

a) What time does your flight leave? ☐

b) The aeroplane will take off at 14:00. ☐

c) Get into the queue quickly. ☐

d) What colour is your nail varnish? ☐

e) Stop doing that! ☐

f) I don't like you. ☐

2. **a)** Write a statement that includes the word daydream.

_____

_____

b) Write a question that includes the word late.

_____

_____

c) Write an imperative that includes the word daffodil.

_____

_____

3. A rhetorical question is one that does not really need an answer,
    e.g. 'I think you should go to bed now Sam, don't you?' said Mum.
    Although it is a question Mum isn't really interested in Sam's opinion.
    Write your own rhetorical question:

_____

_____

_____

Activity

After watching your favourite television programme
or film, try to describe the storyline, briefly, to an adult.
Remember that adults have very short attention spans
so you need to keep them hooked. You can even act bits
out to help them concentrate!

Check Your Progress!
Statements, Questions And Imperatives
Turn to page 48 and put a tick next to what you have just learned.

Parents Start Here...

If your child is good at spotting tenses, you could introduce them to conditionals (could, would) and other past tenses, e.g. I have been/He was playing. See if they can spot the tense while you talk. It helps them understand the sentence and meaning better.

Tenses

Remember!

- A verb written in the present tense tells us that something is happening now, e.g. I am singing, I sing.
- A verb written in the past tense tells us that something has already happened, e.g. I was singing, I sang.
- A verb written in the future tense tells us what will happen, e.g. I will sing, I shall sing.

1. Complete the table below, using the correct tenses. Sometimes you may find that there is more than one possible correct answer:

Past Tense	Present Tense	Future Tense
a) He waited		He will wait
b)	Suzi cooks	
c)		You will pay
d) It broke		
e)	I like you	
f)		They will see me
g)	We buy cakes	

2. Underline the verb in each sentence and state what tense is being used.
The first one has been done for you:

a) Apparently goldfish actually <u>have</u> memories of up to three months. present

b) My radio broke yesterday. _____

c) You will read your name on the notice-board. _____

d) She was hanging the washing out. _____

e) I buy my newspaper on the way home. _____

3. Write a sentence that uses the verb to be in the present tense:

_____

_____

4. Write a sentence that uses the verb to have in the past tense:

_____

_____

5. Write a sentence that uses the verb to go in the future tense:

_____

_____

TRY THIS

Activity

The next time you watch a film think about how the actors make their characters seem convincing.

Check Your Progress!

Tenses ☐

Turn to page 48 and put a tick next to what you have just learned.

Top Tip!
Always look for positive aspects to your child's work as well as helping them to resolve errors.

Parents Start Here...

Your child should now have mastered simple punctuation marks such as capital letters, full stops, commas, question and exclamation marks.

Simple Punctuation

Remember!

- Punctuation marks make a piece of writing easy to read and understand.
- Punctuation adds meaning to a written text.
- You need to be able to identify the different punctuation marks and use them appropriately.

1. Write out these lists using commas:

a) Pens pencils crayons a ruler and a rubber.

_____

b) Gazelles springboks duikers and impala.

_____

c) Muffins cakes biscuits and flapjacks.

_____

2. Write out these sentences, putting in capital letters and full stops:

a) the capital of france is paris

_____

b) ali is my best friend, not joe

_____

c) my favourite singer is robbie williams

_____

3. Turn each sentence into two smaller sentences and punctuate appropriately:

a) three ghostly spectres emerged from the windows of harwood hall they oozed slime and wailed

_____

_____

_____

b) the beaches at eastbourne are famous have you ever been there

_____

_____

_____

c) dad loves watching james bond movies he loves the action drama and scenery

_____

_____

_____

 Activity

Write your own play and invite some friends to help you act it out.

Check Your Progress!
Simple Punctuation
Turn to page 48 and put a tick next to what you have just learned.

Top Tip!
If your child loses concentration here, let them take a break.

Parents Start Here...

Children are awarded extra marks in SATs for the appropriate use of more complex punctuation and for employing varied vocabulary.

Punctuation: Semicolons And Colons

Remember!

- Semicolons are used to join two phrases that could stand alone as sentences, e.g. The headteacher's door is always open; you can walk in any time.
- The second phrase often gives you more detail or information about the first phrase.
- Colons are used to introduce a list of items, e.g. We use three types of renewable energy: solar, wind and hydropower.

1. Join the two sentences using semicolons:

a) Jane ran down the road. She did not want to miss the bus.

b) Elephants like to lounge in mud. It cools them down.

c) Crisps are very fattening. They are covered in oil.

d) It is good to eat lots of fish. They are high in protein but low in fat.

e) All bicycles should have mudguards. They protect your clothes from spray.

2. Write these lists out using colons and commas:

a) There are different types of egg free range barn organic and battery.

_____

_____

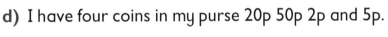

b) The boy sang the song several ways loudly slowly softly and sadly.

_____

_____

c) I can knit anything gloves hats scarves socks and even vests.

_____

_____

d) I have four coins in my purse 20p 50p 2p and 5p.

_____

_____

Activity

There are other places where you might use colons, to introduce a quotation for example. Look out for these in your reading.

Check Your Progress!
Punctuation: Semicolons And Colons
Turn to page 48 and put a tick next to what you have just learned.

Top Tip!
If your child struggles with anything, don't worry – let them go at their own pace.

Parents Start Here...

Learning new words helps to enrich a child's vocabulary, increases their comprehension skills and improves the quality of their writing.

Collective Nouns

Remember!

- Collective nouns are given to groups of things or people.
- Some collective nouns, such as herd, are well-known. Others, such as charm, are more unusual.

1. Choose the best collective noun to complete the phrases:

crowd   fleet   choir   collection   herd   shoal

a) a _____ of ships

b) a _____ of singers

c) a _____ of stamps

d) a _____ of fish

e) a _____ of people

f) a _____ of cows

2. Complete the phrases:

a) a bunch of _____

b) a library of _____

c) a forest of _____

d) a pride of _____

e) an army of _____

f) a flock of _____

3. Use a dictionary to complete these collective nouns:

a) a plague of _____

b) a brood of _____

c) a bench of _____

d) a charm of _____

TRY THIS   Activity

Suggest that all the members of your family discuss a particular topic at a mealtime. It could be an important decision that needs to be made or something in the news. Who is the best listener? Who puts their opinions forward most convincingly?

Check Your Progress!

Collective Nouns ☐

Turn to page 48 and put a tick next to what you have just learned.

Top Tip! Learning is fun, so if your child is tired, let them come back to this when they are fresh.

Parents Start Here...

When Year Six children are able to write complex sentences they are writing at an appropriate level for their age group.

Sentence Structure

Remember!

- Simple sentences have only one verb, e.g. The cat sat on the mat.
- Compound sentences are made up of more than one simple sentence. The simple sentences are often joined by a conjunctive, e.g. The cat sat on the mat and then it was sick.
- Complex sentences are compound sentences in which one part depends on another, e.g. The cat was really sick because it had eaten two mice.

1. Write four simple sentences:

1. _____

2. _____

3. _____

4. _____

2. Write three compound sentences:

1. _____

2. _____

3. _____

3. Write two complex sentences:

1. _____

_____

2. _____

_____

4. Identify each sentence as simple, compound or complex:

a) My pet elephant tore his ear
and had to be taken to the vet.   _____

b) I have a pet elephant.   _____

c) My pet elephant tore his ear
because it got caught in the car door.   _____

d) She told him off.   _____

e) She told him off when he arrived late
to the lesson for the third time that week.   _____

f) She told him off as he walked in late.   _____

 Activity

Pick a poem that you particularly enjoy. Learn it off by heart
and then recite it to a small audience; see if they enjoy it too.

Check Your Progress!
Sentence Structure ☐
Turn to page 48 and put a tick next to what you have just learned.

29

Parents Start Here...

It is acceptable to use single or double speech marks. Children are most frequently taught to use the double form, to avoid confusion with apostrophes. Also try to encourage your child to avoid using "said" and think of more imaginative words.

Direct Speech

Remember!

- Direct speech is when we write down the exact words someone has spoken.
- We use speech marks, or inverted commas, to show direct speech, e.g. "hello" she said.
- Punctuation like question marks or exclamation marks should go inside the speech marks, e.g "Help!" he yelled.

1. Complete the sentence, putting in what you think the person might be saying. Use the correct punctuation:

a) _____

_____ the man said.

b) _____

_____ the little boy asked.

c) _____

_____ the old man yelled.

2. Write these sentences out, adding speech marks:

a) His aunt said I would prefer to sit there.

b) Don't jump yet! shouted the man.

c) I haven't decided, said the woman, I like them both.

d) Do you know what the time is? enquired the security guard.

e) No one loves me, the D. J. joked.

 Activity

Find out what a dialogue is.
When you know, have a go at writing one of your own.

Check Your Progress!
Direct Speech
Turn to page 48 and put a tick next to what you have just learned.

Top Tip!
Always look for positive aspects to your child's work as well as helping them to resolve errors.

Parents Start Here...

Encourage your child to study how dialogue is written in books and newspapers. Newspapers use reported speech and you may need to ask your child to tell you how reported and direct speech differ. This will show their understanding.

Reported Speech

Remember!

- Reported speech is when we write about what someone said without writing the exact words.
- You do not need to use speech marks for reported speech, e.g. She told me that she won't eat meringue.

1. Change these sentences so they use reported speech.
   The first one has been done for you:

a) Mo said "I like toffee".
   Mo said that she likes toffee.

b) The waiter called "get me more coffee".

c) Emily said "I am scared of walking over bridges".

d) Neil Armstrong said "this is a giant leap for mankind".

e) "Would you like a little more trimmed off?" the hairdresser asked me.

2. Change these sentences from reported speech to direct speech. The first one has been done for you:

a) Denis said that Ted could not go the youth club.
   "You cannot go to the youth club, Ted" said Denis.

b) Mum told me that she missed the 6 o'clock train.

_____

c) The doctor politely called to the Nurse for more oxygen.

_____

d) The hopeful singer declared that he is going to be a star.

_____

e) The workman yelled at Mike, telling him to dig a little further.

_____

 Activity

Try to write your own newspaper report using reported speech. Remember to think about what, when, where and how something happened. Your interviews with witnesses will need reported speech.

Check Your Progress!
                    Reported Speech
Turn to page 48 and put a tick next to what you have just learned.

Top Tip! Remember to give your child lots of praise – they will work so much better.

Parents Start Here...

Your child has learnt lots of rules concerning grammar but it only makes sense when put into practice. Ensure your child carries their skills over into every piece of written work they do.

Organising Your Work

Remember!

- A group of sentences that are about the same subject is called a paragraph.
- Start a new line every time you begin a paragraph.
- Leave a space at the beginning of the first line in a paragraph. This is an indent.
- Paragraphs help break up a piece of writing.
- Start a new line every time a new person speaks when you are writing direct speech (dialogue).

Edit this piece of writing. Write it out in the space provided. • Use paragraphs where necessary. • Correct spellings. • Improve the punctuation. • Ask an adult to check your finished piece of work.• Continue the story (you can tell the story or write it).

There are few things more frightening than an empty house especially one that has been uninhabited for a number of years it was just such a house that the twins lucy and george had to walk past every day as they climbed the hill to skhool. The talk in the village was of a crazy young man who had murdered his hole familly in the house but no one new the real facts it was all just gossip. But the truth did not matter to the children. All they new was that the house emitted a fowl stench, torn fabric could be seen moving in the windows and doors could be heard slamming when the wind was high. One day, as they returned from school, the twins saw a 'sold' sign posted outside the house a van drew up alongside them and out stepped a ...

_____

_____

_____

_____

_____

_____

_____

_____

_____

_____

_____

_____

_____

_____

_____

_____

_____

_____

TRY THIS

Activity

Checking and amending your work is an important skill.
Try to look over every piece of work you complete;
there are always things you can improve.

Check Your Progress!
Organising Your Work ☐
Turn to page 48 and put a tick next to what you have just learned.

Top Tip!
If your child loses concentration here, let them take a break.

Parents Start Here...

Words that end in s can show ownership by either adding 's or just the apostrophe, e.g. Puss's paw is sore/ Puss' paw is sore. Let your child continue with whichever method they have been taught at school.

Showing Ownership

Remember!

- **Apostrophes** are used to show that something belongs to somebody.
- The position of the apostrophe is very important because it can change the meaning:

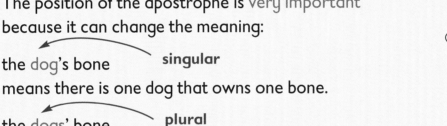

the dog's bone   **singular**

means there is one dog that owns one bone.

the dogs' bone   **plural**

means that two or more dogs own the bone.

- When you have a collective noun treat it like a singular noun, not a plural, e.g. The pack's leader was a large male.
- Remember there is only one pack, so it is a singular noun.

1. Write out these phrases using apostrophes to show ownership. The first one has been done for you:

a) The shoes of Sean → Sean's shoes

b) The room of Stanley _____

c) The biscuit of Adrian _____

d) The book of Wimbledon Library _____

e) The eggs of Doris _____

2. These sentences contain plurals and ownership words.
Put the apostrophes in the correct places:

a) We sat upon the camels backs and rode over the hills.

b) They hid the childrens clothes.

c) You will find the girls sweatshirts at the end of their beds.

d) I went into the ladies loo by mistake.

e) All of the bottles labels are missing.

f) Three quarters of the herds calves are sick.

g) Some of the rabbits tails are white, others are brown.

 Activity

Most children (and lots of adults) find apostrophes tricky.
Be sure you can do the questions on these pages before you
move on to look at contractions.

Check Your Progress!
Showing Ownership
Turn to page 48 and put a tick next to what you have just learned.

37

Parents Start Here...

Discourage your child from using contractions in formal written work. It is perfectly acceptable in informal writing and for written speech.

Contractions

Remember!

- Apostrophes are used to show missing letters in words that have been shortened.
- Shortened words are called contractions.
- The apostrophe replaces one or more letters.

1. Write each sentence using a contraction instead:

a) We are going to the park.

_____

b) I do not know the answer.

_____

c) They will come tomorrow.

_____

d) There is a fair on the green.

_____

e) I would have gone with you.

_____

2. Write out these contractions in full:

a) couldn't   _____

b) shouldn't   _____

c) let's   _____

d) isn't   _____

e) haven't   _____

f) shan't   _____

g) I'm   _____

h) we've   _____

i) who's   _____

j) you've   _____

k) I'd   _____

Activity

Won't, like shan't, is a rather unusual contraction. Do you know what it is short for?

Check Your Progress!

Contractions ☐

Turn to page 48 and put a tick next to what you have just learned.

Top Tip!
If your child struggles with anything, don't worry – let them go at their own pace.

Parents Start Here...

Do not move on from this page until you are confident your child can determine when to use its and when to use it's. Many adults remain confused by this difference, so be patient and support your child until they fully understand this.

Its And It's

Remember!

- You must learn when to use its and when to use it's.
- Its is a pronoun, just like his or hers. Pronouns never have an apostrophe to show ownership because the word is already doing that, e.g. his mouth, her mouth , its mouth.
- It's is a contraction and it is short for 'it is', e.g. it's a cat = it is a cat.
- If you are not sure whether to use an apostrophe or not then say 'it is' instead of its. If it makes sense you should use an apostrophe, e.g. its mine → it is mine → use an apostrophe → it's mine.

1. Use the correct form of its/it's:

a) The lemming lost _____ nerve when it peered over the edge of the cliff.

b) _____ the straw that broke the camel's back.

c) The story of how the zebra lost _____ spots.

d) The polish has come off _____ surface.

e) The circus has lost some of _____ appeal.

f) I don't like _____ new tyres – they make the car look strange.

g) _____ not the first time, and it won't be the last.

h) _____ the time of year for unsettled weather.

2. Write each sentence but write the contraction out in full.
The first one has been done for you:

a) It's the summer.
It is the summer.

b) It's my hat.

_____

c) That is why it's broken.

_____

d) That is just the way it's going to be.

_____

3. Tick the correct punctuation:

  a) The cat has lots its ball. ☐

  b) The cat has lots it's ball. ☐

  c) Its going to be a great party. ☐

  d) It's going to be a great party. ☐

  e) The kite lost it's tail. ☐

  f) The kite lost its tail. ☐

Activity

Look in shops, at notices and even official letters and you will find that many adults are ignorant of the rules regarding it's and its. Make it your mission not to be like them.

Check Your Progress!

Its And It's ☐

Turn to page 48 and put a tick next to what you have just learned.

Top Tip!
Learning is fun, so if your child is tired, let them come back to this when they are fresh.

Parents Start Here...

Help your child plan their piece of written work before they start writing. The whole task should take no longer than 45 minutes, including planning time.

Practise Writing

Remember!

- Use some of the writing skills you have revised so far. You can write fiction or non-fiction. Choose from a heading:
  Friends
  Ten Years From Now
  Fire
  Run For Your Life
- Use the space on the rest of this page for your plan:

Plan

Start your writing here:

Activity

Make sure you have a strong beginning and end to your piece of writing. Try to make it interesting for the reader. Remember to break your writing up into paragraphs. Use as many interesting words as you can. Check your punctuation and spelling.

Check Your Progress!

Practise Writing ☐

Turn to page 48 and put a tick next to what you have just learned.

Answers

Pages 4–5
1. I do not understand why my <u>daughter</u>, **Maggie**, cannot put her dirty <u>laundry</u> into the <u>basket</u>. Every <u>day</u> I go into her <u>bedroom</u> and I never know what I will find. On **Tuesday Maggie** had left a wet <u>towel</u> on the <u>carpet</u>, which was soggy and smelly by **Wednesday**. On **Thursday** I found an old <u>mug</u> under **Maggie's** <u>bed</u>. It was harbouring some <u>fungus</u> I think. I've had a good <u>idea</u> though. I am sending **Maggie** to work for **Joyce**, a <u>friend</u> of mine who runs a cleaning <u>company</u>. Hopefully she will get the <u>hint</u>.
2. a) Denmark
b) Sweden
c) Russia
d) Wales
e) Ireland
f) Italy
g) China
h) South Africa
i) Austria
j) Spain

Pages 6–7
1. a) cranky; old; knobbly
b) wooden; porcelain
c) lazy; messy
d) pink; pink; pink; pink

Pages 8–9
1. a) blew; making
b) was raised; slipped
c) plucked; tearing
d) peered; spotted; lying
3. a) past
b) future
c) past
d) present
e) future
4. a) were
b) was
c) will be
d) is

Pages 10–11
1. a) quickly
b) brightly
c) tenderly
d) angrily
e) well
3. a) wonderfully
b) possibly
c) originally
d) wisely
e) happily
f) simply
g) nicely

Pages 12–13
1. The ancient Indian Snake Charmer sat <u>upon</u> his lavishly embroidered cushion. There were tiny silver bells sewn <u>around</u> the edges of the cushion and they tinkled every time he moved. <u>Before</u> him was a large raffia basket. <u>Inside</u> the basket something moved. The Snake Charmer looked <u>beneath</u> the lid and leapt back in surprise...
2. b) Noun: frog; lily-pad
Verb: leapt
Adjective: young
Preposition: over
c) Proper Noun: Fluffy
Noun: shed
Verb: was buried
Adjective: new
Preposition: next to
d) Noun: goblins; mountain
Verb: dug
Preposition: below
e) Noun: train; tunnel
Verb: came
Adverb: noisily
Adjective (2): dark, gloomy
Preposition: out of

Pages 14–15
1. a) My name is John and I am 10 years old.
b) I stamped on the dolly so hard it broke.
c) Harriet is my sister and she often teases me.
d) The pigeons flew overhead and they made a terrible noise.
e) The horrid boy chewed his gum then he spat it on to the road.

Pages 16–17
1. a) because
b) and
c) but
d) until
e) if
2. Suitable conjunctions might be 'and', 'before', 'then', 'but', etc.
3. a) The
b) an
c) some
4. As <u>the</u> children emerged through <u>the</u> silvery cloud they saw <u>an</u> amazing sight. <u>Some</u> sparks of light flew around their heads and, as <u>a</u> gentle breeze tickled their faces, <u>a</u> golden face appeared in front of them.

Pages 18–19
1. Questions: (a) and (d)
Imperatives: (c) and (e)
Statements: (b) and (f)

Pages 20–21
1.

Past Tense	Present Tense	Future Tense
a) He waited	He waits	He will wait
b) Suzi cooked	Suzi cooks	Suzi wil cook
c) You paid	You pay	You will pay
d) It broke	It breaks	It will break
e) I liked you	I like you	I will like you
f) They saw me	They see me	They will see me
g) We bought cakes	We buy cakes	We will buy cakes

You may have written phrases like 'is waiting' or 'did buy'; these are also acceptable answers.
2. b) broke (past)
c) will read (future)
d) was hanging (past)
e) buy (present)

Answers

Pages 22–23
1. a) Pens, pencils, crayons, a ruler and a rubber.
b) Gazelles, springboks, duikers and impala.
c) Muffins, cakes, biscuits and flapjacks.
2. a) The capital of France is Paris.
b) Ali is my best friend, not Joe.
c) My favourite singer is Robbie Williams.
3. a) Three ghostly spectres emerged from the windows of Harwood Hall. They oozed slime and wailed.
b) The beaches at Eastbourne are famous. Have you ever been there?
c) Dad loves watching James Bond movies. He loves the action, drama and scenery.

Pages 24–25
1. a) Jane ran down the road; she did not want to miss the bus.
b) Elephants like to lounge in mud; it cools them down.
c) Crisps are very fattening; they are covered in oil.
d) It is good to eat lots of fish; they are high in protein but low in fat.
e) All bicycles should have mudguards; they protect your clothes from spray.
2. a) There are different types of egg: free range, barn, organic and battery.
b) The boy sang the song several ways: loudly, slowly, softly and sadly.
c) I can knit anything: gloves, hats, scarves, socks and even vests.
d) I have four coins in my purse: 20p, 50p, 2p and 5p.

Pages 26–27
1. a) fleet
b) choir
c) collection
d) shoal
e) crowd
f) herd
2. a) flowers/grapes/bananas
b) books
c) trees
d) lions
e) soldiers
f) birds

Pages 28–29
4. a) compound
b) simple
c) complex
d) simple
e) complex
f) compound

Pages 30–31
2. a) His aunt said "I would prefer to sit there."
b) "Don't jump yet!" shouted the man.
c) "I haven't decided," said the woman, "I like them both."
d) "Do you know what the time is?" enquired the security guard.
e) "No one loves me," the D. J. joked.

Pages 32–33
1. b) The waiter called for more coffee.
c) Emily said she was scared of walking over bridges.
d) Neil Armstrong said it was a giant leap for mankind.
e) The hairdresser asked me if I would like (or wanted) a little more trimmed off.
2. b) "I missed the 6 o'clock train" said Mum.
c) "Oxygen, please Nurse" called the doctor.
d) "I am going to be a star" declared the hopeful singer.
e) The workman yelled "just dig a little further, Mike!"

Pages 36–37
1. b) Stanley's room
c) Adrian's biscuit
d) Wimbledon Library's book
e) Doris's (or Doris') eggs.
2. a) We sat upon the camels' backs and rode over the hills.
b) They hid the children's clothes.
c) You will find the girls' sweatshirts at the end of their beds.
d) I went into the ladies' loo by mistake.
e) All of the bottles' labels are missing.
f) Three quarters of the herd's calves are sick.
g) Some of the rabbits' tails are white, others are brown.

Pages 38–39
1. a) We're going to the park.
b) I don't know the answer.
c) They'll come tomorrow.
d) There's a fair on the green.
e) I'd have gone with you **or** I would've gone with you.
2. a) could not
b) should not
c) let us
d) is not
e) have not
f) shall not
g) I am
h) we have
i) who is
j) you have
k) I would

Pages 40–41
1. a) its
b) It's
c) its
d) its
e) its
f) its
g) It's
h) It's
2. b) It is my hat.
c) That is why it is broken.
d) That is just the way it is going to be.
3. a), d) and f) are all correct.

Check Your Progress!

Nouns ....

Adjectives ....

Verbs ....

Adverbs ....

Prepositions ....

Pronouns..

Conjunctions And Articles ....

Statements, Questions And Imperatives ....

Tenses ....

Simple Punctuation ....

Punctuation: Semicolons And Colons ....

Collective Nouns ....

Sentence Structure ....

Direct Speech ....

Reported Speech ....

Organising Your Work ....

Showing Ownership...

Contractions..

Its And It's..

Practise Writing ....